Winter

by Tanya Thayer

Lerner Books · London · New York · Minneapolis

It is winter.

It is cold.

The days are short.

Most trees do not
have leaves.

Dormice sleep.

People stay warm.

Foxes **hunt** for food.

People eat warm food.

Lakes **freeze.**

People skate.

Animals have warm coats.

People have warm clothes.

Animals dig for food.

Icicles start to **melt.**

Sap starts to **flow** from trees.

Spring is coming.

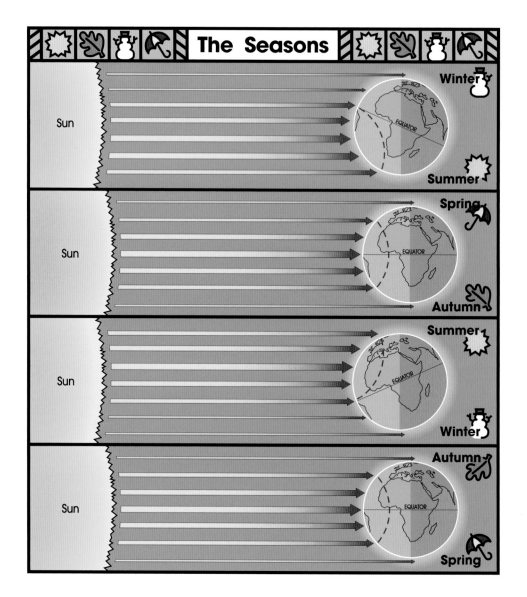

18

Seasons

The Earth moves around the Sun. The Sun shines on the Earth. When the Sun shines mostly on the southern half of the Earth, it is summer there. But it is winter in the northern half of the Earth. When the Sun shines mostly on the northern half of the Earth, it is winter in the southern half.

There is less sunlight in the winter than there is in the autumn. The days are shorter too. When there is less sunlight in a day, it is colder.

Winter Facts

In some parts of the world it feels like winter all year long.

Some animals grow white fur or feathers in the winter. Animals that are white are harder to see in the snow. They are camouflaged in the snow.

Food is harder for animals to find in the winter. Some animals cannot find enough food to live.

Trees that do not have leaves in the winter are dormant. Dormant means that the tree does not grow. The dormant tree will grow again in the spring.

Some animals stay warm and healthy by sleeping in a den all winter. Animals that sleep all winter are hibernating.

Glossary

 flow – to move in a stream

 freeze – when a liquid gets very cold and turns into a solid

 hunt – to look for food

 melt – when a solid becomes warm and turns into a liquid

 sap – the liquid inside a plant

Index

This book was first published in the United States of America in 2002.

First published in the United Kingdom in 2008 by
Lerner Books,
Dalton House,
60 Windsor Avenue,
London SW19 2RR

Website address: www.lernerbooks.co.uk

This edition was updated and edited for UK publication by Discovery Books Ltd.,
Unit 3, 37 Watling Street, Leintwardine, Shropshire SY7 0LW

Words in **bold** type are explained in the glossary on page 22.

British Library Cataloguing in Publication Data

Thayer, Tanya
    Winter. - (First step non-fiction. Seasons)
    1. Winter - Juvenile literature
    I. Title
    508.2

    ISBN-13: 978 1 58013 385 2

The photographs in this book are reproduced through the courtesy of:
©Robert Fried/robertfriedphotography.com, front cover; ©National Science Foundation, p 2; ©John R Kreul/Independent Picture Service, p 3; ©John Kohout/Root Resources, p 4; ©Stephen Graham Photography p 5; ©George McCarthy/Corbis, p 6; ©Danny Lehman/Corbis, p 7; ©Michele Burgess, pp 8, 22 (middle); ©Corbis, p 9; ©Stephen G Donaldson, pp 10, 22 (second from top); ©Cardiff City Council, p 11; ©Paulette Johnson, p 12; ©Joseph Sohm; ChromoSohm Inc./Corbis, p 13; ©Ed Kashi, p 14; ©Richard Cummins, pp 15, 22 (second from bottom); ©D Richter MTV/Visuals Unlimited, pp 16, 22 (top, bottom); ©D Yeske/Visuals Unlimited, p 17.

Printed in China